Love Letters to a Ghost Named C

Adam Levon Brown

Madness Muse Press

Cover Design by Adam Levon Brown

Madness Muse Press
420 Autumn Ave
Eugene, Oregon 97404

www.MadnessMusePress.com

Madness Muse Press

Table of Contents

Foreword

Coming soon!

That Girl in the Tie-Dye Muscle Shirt

I started the day off like I would any
other.
I ignored the alarm and got to
Springfield High school
2 hours late.

I ate my lunch alone and wandered
off campus for
a cigarette. I walked back in time for
gym class.
Little did I know that this class
wouldn't come close to
being anything like I'd ever
experienced.

There she was…

About 5' 3", long black hair, a smile
that could convince
a banker to leave his job for
housecleaning. She wore cut-off

shorts and a tie-dye muscle shirt. She
was muscular and cute.

I, having no experience with any
knowledge of flirtation, just watched
her
I knew she was special. There
seemed to be a light emanating
around her.

I put the ideas I had in the back of
my mind and went along with
running
the circuit around the gym. I smoked,
but I could run.

God could I run.

I was always walking or running
somewhere;
perhaps trying to escape my
problems.

Broken home, mom on drugs,

parents separated, same old story.

As I took each breath and passed
student after student, I was building
courage in asking the Halo-engulfed
girl her name.

The gym instructor blew his whistle
and demanded that we sit and
stretch.
We walked to our assigned places on
the gym floor and sat.

As I was doing the butterfly stretch, I
looked at her again.

HOLY SHIT!

She was looking back!

I didn't know how to handle that
kind of attention and became one
large nerve
which kept being pricked with barbs

from a cactus.

I walked up to her after her class and
mumbled,

"What is your name?"

Her luminous smile set me at ease.
and she said.

"My name is C."

Destiny? Or Coincidence?

The same day that we introduced
ourselves to each other,
I ran into her in what the school
called, "The Smoking Corner."
It's where all the "Bad" types hung
out to do drugs and smoke
cigarettes.

They eventually got a cop to patrol
the area, but that's a different story.

I ran into her smile and was
flabbergasted enough to take a step
back.
I looked nervously down at my shoes
and mumbled to her in my most
eloquent way of
speaking.

"Want a cig?"

She took the cigarette out of my

hand and lit it up.
We started talking about this and
that, that and this.

School was over and she was still
with me.
This surprised the hell out of me.

We started walking down Centennial
avenue still rambling on
about how fucked up school was;
about how we would soon be
free.
I relaxed a bit and asked her if she
wanted to go the park.
By my utter astonishment she said
yes.

I could feel the sweat start to form on
my neck again, as I awkwardly
walked beside her like a Wildebeest
    in a Lion's den.

We got to the park and played on the

swings awhile.

I felt like I was a toddler again.

Highschool had been

a non-stop ram-jam of hornets to the

face,

and this was the best that I had felt in

a long time.

By nightfall, she was still there.

Never had I had this kind of

attention before from a girl.

For the first time since my 10th

    birthday, I formed a real smile.

The night was young and I could feel

    the flow of darkness

on my cheek.

I chose to embrace it.

The First Night

I remember the time we drank with
those winos in
front of the cannon war memorial at
Willamalane Park.

We were stupid kids with nothing to
lose.

The Cherry Blossom trees enveloped
us with
hopscotch dreams and real scotch
hangovers.

I remember our first night together in
the same park.

We huddled against a fence while
watching a toy light saber battle
between two friends.

What she didn't
know was that the real

light show was evolving in my chest.
THU-THUMP
THU-THUMP
THU-THUMP

My heart was going to explode!

It was the first time I ever sat with
a girl on my lap.
I was 15 years old and the world was
careless and undaunting.
The Juniper moon spit its seeds of
light around our feet as the
night quickened to a roaring
applause.

I was crushed between her and the
fence but not
wanting to ruin the moment,
I bore the pain. I was 15 and thought
I could tear steel apart,
what was a little back pain?
THU-THUMP
THU-THUMP

THU-THUMP

The night ended with my first French
    kiss.
I had no idea what I was doing,
I let her steer my tongue since
I was a paralyzed eel
on her fisher's boat.
I didn't care.

It felt good and I was going
to experience it for as long as
possible. My jaw felt like a
ton of potatoes that night while
walking home alone. I hoped
and prayed that it was only the
    beginning.

Stars in Your Eyes

Fast forward one month
We were officially a couple
and the sun shined on me with
all of its praise for the first time in my life.
Waking up every day was an exciting
journey.

I would awaken to a nibble on my ear,
someone sitting on me, or someone
laughing.

She was heavily into skating, so our first
weeks together were spent at a skateboard
shop
called Sk8ers. The display model of a
skateboard
was in place for people to practice their
moves.

Just to emphasize how bad my injury was,
I was bed-ridden for week
I walked up to that board like I was

Tarzan and ready to slide along the trees.

I tried an Ollie and the board slipped
from underneath me as if I was one of the
Mario Brothers being swept away by an
angry turtle.

I landed on the cement floor underneath and
wondered
what the hell had just happened.

She laughed and laughed and laughed.

The pain was excruciating, but my ego took
the biggest punch.

 I hobbled over to the couch and she
followed behind.
While nursing my shrunken head, she
initiated a kiss.
The fireworks from the movie, "Mulan"
exploded into my head.
While drunk on dopamine, I decided to try
to say something romantic.

All that came from my mouth was,

"You have stars in your eyes"

Damn I was good.

I knew that at any moment, we would be off
to my parents' apartment to begin making
out.

This wasn't the case.

She laughed even harder than when I fell
and I sat there awkward, with a face full of
ketchup embarrassment.
I quickly changed the subject and asked if
she wanted to go eat.

She wore a smile that seemed to say, "God,
I'm with an idiot, but he's sweet."
We left to the Mcdonald's down the road.
She walked, while I strutted along like a
geriatric
pool of sweat.

Sweaty Palms Forever

Another month or two rolls by
with Halcyon slickness

We were seeing each other
almost every day

We played video games a lot as I had the
brand new
Playstation 1 in my possession. I thought to
myself devilishly,

"This will keep her here."

I was an avid gamer and my reflexes were as
fine-tuned
as clocks in a Victorian Watch-makers shop.
I would lose a lot, which pissed me off.

But having her there was the real prize, so
I let it go.

She would always make jokes and the
occasional
sexual remark which would leave my palms
sweaty
and unable to maneuver the game controller.

She was a master of psychology,
A gaming queen of the 2000's

She knew what I wanted and she
used it against me.

I was a helpless "newbie" in the limelight
of a seasoned chef of sexual innuendo.

She knew what she was doing,
but I didn't;
I never really have.

She pummeled me again and again
on the Playstation 1 at pretty much every
game

Finally, one day, I decided to try to be sneaky.

I put vegetable oil on her controller to level the playing field.

AHA!
I had done it!

Today was my day and no one could take it from me!
Except her that is.

Right before we started to play the game,"
Siphon filter,"
She said she was sick of playing video games.

We went to the park that day.

I still hold that grudge.

Kicked out of High School

As I mention these times that C and I shared,
I must admit that we were both skipping
large
amounts of school.

The truancy officer came to my door many
times
and every time I would become the perfect
child.

"Yes, sir"

"Yes, I agree with you, kids should be in
school."

"I am turning my life around, I have seen the
error of my ways."

One day while I was walking to school, I
decided to stop
by the smoking corner to see if any of my
friendly acquaintances

were there.

C stopped me by holding her hand in front
of my chest.
She took a bottle out of her pocket and said,
"Smell this"

I knew what it was.
It was some good marijuana by the smell of
it.

We hid in the bushes and smoked what was
probably
a 5 sack.

I was as high as doves in Heaven.

We laughed and made jokes.

In our supreme intelligence, we decided to
take a stroll
around the High School campus

We were quickly swallowed up by one of
the school's
security guards.

My heart was racing and I felt like passing
out.

SHIT! HE IS GOING TO KNOW I'M
HIGH!

The security guard casually walked us
towards
the Principal's office where he told us to
have a seat.

The waiting
Oh God, the waiting.

Paranoid thoughts began to blister my
opened mind.

"I'm going to jail, I'm going to Jail."
"

The principal asked us to take a seat and she
began moving her lips.
I could barely see straight, let alone figure
out what she was trying to say to us.

Finally, the peanuts fell into place and I
heard three words,

Expulsion for truancy

We smelled like Columbian drug lords but
they didn't even mention that, though
reflecting back I'm sure they noticed it.

The day ended with getting grounded.
The weeks without C and the news of
expulsion weighed on me like a freight of
dead fish.
I waited in fear for my Dad to kick my ass to
the next planet
I stayed low and clear of him, hiding out in
my room for at least
a week after that.

The following week lightened up like an
Easter Egg on Christmas
and I began to feel better about myself.

This is when the real trouble began...

That Time We Almost Robbed Wal-Mart

C and I hung out in the seediest parts of
town in the Devil's hours.
We would always be looking for new ways
to have fun, get high, get in trouble.

One ominous night of the red harvest moon
we were outside of a Jasper's smoke shop
asking for money to buy a pack of cigs to
split

We were underage, so the person would
have had to physically purchase them as
well.

One lady we talked to mentioned that Wal-
Mart kept their bottles and cans behind the
store
She also told us that it was possible to swipe
them and return them for cash at another
place.

Now this was the fun challenge I was waiting for.

We walked like panthers on a hunt through the darkened streets until we reached Wal-mart.
We talked it up as we were prowling, pumping ourselves up for the grand heist.

When we reached Wal-mart around Three AM, we noticed no one around and so we snuck
to the back of the store and saw our prize.

An entire dumpster full of cans and bottles just waiting to be sold

I quickly noticed the security cameras and backed off before I was in view of them.
C started walking towards the cans.

"STOP! CAMERAS!" I yelled to her.

We stood there ready to risk arrest for about
10 minutes all for a quick nicotine fix.

Fear inched its way along my spine as sweat
formed on my naked face.

We repeatedly called each other pussies
since neither of us would dare show the
camera
our face.

We backed off.

We walked back towards Jasper's with
defeat in our eyes, and a nicotine fit so
strong
that we were starting to nag at each other.

Just as we thought that there was no
prevailing in the situation,
we noticed a pack left with two cigarettes
sitting in the ashtray outside
of Jasper's.

We smoked like kings at the creek near my
apartment that night and fell asleep huddling
in the cold like two Carmel cracker jacks
stuck together

Jealousy is Not a Virtue

"C" had many friends in all levels of places.
She brought some of them to my parents'
apartment.
One in particular I hated simply because I
knew
that C liked him.

Feelings of insecurity led to malicious
thoughts about
acting against this person.

So many thoughts ran through my whirlwind
mind.

I should smash up his car with a bat.
I should punch him in the face.
I should go to his home and break his
windows.

I was always pissed when she brought him
around

My jealousy led to alcohol and alcohol led
to many
arguments with C.

I was a drunken mess and made myself look
like a fool.

One time in particular, she showed up at my
doorstep with him
and I just lost it.

I yelled at them both and told C to get the
fuck out of here.
To my surprise, she did.

I thought I had lost her forever at that
moment.
I decided to go around to our spots and look
for her.

Before I left, I wrote a poem for her to try to
make up for what I'd done....

"Banshee

Losing you is something
I've regretted since primitive times.

Neanderthalic instincts of jealousy
and pride burned

the love you held for me
in a Salem-style pyre.

Bouts of alcohol-induced
anger blinded me while

scattering the ashes of
our love to the wild winds of indifference.

I slipped and fell
heart-first out of your life.
My descent quickened while I notched a
mark
inside the chipped Ruby of your chest.

I landed on my sorrow;
Emotional scar-

That no longer bleeds,
but screams your name

every time I touch it."

I took the poem and folded it into my wallet.

I found her near the school we'd been
previously expelled from
walking with two other guys.

These guys I knew not to fuck with since
they were both about twice
my size.

And so I followed like a twisted angry
puppy at the heel of its owner.
It didn't occur to me that C was upset and
that I should just leave her alone for awhile.

I went home eventually and waited.
Waited
and waited

She eventually came back and I apologized
immediately.
We made out that night on my parents bed
when they were away.
I'll never forget that day because I learned
that a part of me is not so easy going.

I think she forgave me because she never
mentioned it.
I crumpled the poem up and threw it away.

The colors were splattered against the
canvas of life again.
I was able to sleep soundly that night.

The Apartment

C and I spent a lot of time at Hallmark Apartments where my parents lived. My Parents were always busy so we were pretty much left to do whatever we wanted. We smoked up my mom's cigarettes, drank my dad's beer, roughhoused, and anything you can imagine. The place was a small hazard zone because we never cleaned.

Loud music and long laughs permeated the days and nights. It's as if I was in a dream world that was made just for me.

I was a total shut-in and she was very outgoing. She got me out of the apartment and into a light-yielding world of magic.

Fun was never in short supply as we found multitudes of ways to have fun, sometimes at the expense of others.

Our favorite game was to walk by strangers and talk about something either perverted or just outlandish. One time I talked in the voice of Gollum from Lord of The Rings while walking past a construction worker.

"Myyyyyy Precccccccciiiiiiousssss"

The man in the orange and white reflective vest didn't know what to think while he shook his head and began focusing again on his work.

Another game we played was the screaming game. We would go to West Moreland Park and scream as loud as we could. The final time we played, a police officer came up to us and told us that neighbors 2 miles away were complaining of noise in the area. We stopped after that, but it still amazes me that our voices carried that far. Perhaps it was the strength of our lungs, or maybe, just maybe, some kind of Banshee possessed us for a little while.

Many Days at McDonald's

C got a job at McDonald's restaurant just a block away from my parents' apartment. She loved it and I could tell. She always wanted to get a job but was, until then, too young to work. I often stopped by for a McChicken sandwich and a large Coca-Cola. Every time I saw her, she always had a smile on her face. After work, she would stop by and we would hang out. She complained of coughing bouts and feeling tired a lot. I always thought it was the cigarettes, so I never said anything. She was almost always in a joyful state of mind and would crack jokes often. Squeezing her hands to her cheeks to imitate her face stuck against a bus window.

"Mr. Bus driver, can you please open the door?"

I laughed and laughed.

She was filled with a good spirit and great
sense.

We fooled around a lot, and you can blame
that on the teenage hormones.

There were many nights of passionate kisses
and the promise of tomorrow.
We were young

 I saw the universe and I was never going to
look away.

The Engagement

It was a tempered summer morning, pitch
black, at the apartment around 3 AM.
I got this crazy idea in my brain and decided
to risk everything.

But let me back up.

C and I had decided to go camping outside
that night. The air was thin and the
temperature was warm. We were going to
stay outside the apartment and catch nature
in its true skin.

We watched some poorly dubbed anime on
TV and talked for awhile while smoking the
last of our Camel Cigarettes.

We talked about the moon, the stars,
extraterrestrial life, and most notably, what
we were going to eat.

That night, I decided to propose to her. I was
an excited lightning bolt of sweat as I
fumbled around the apartment looking for
jewelry to use.

I finally settled on a cheap copper ring that I
had gotten in a box of cereal. I was
extremely poor and had only this to offer.

I stuffed it down into my bottomless pocket
where I kept everything else and asked her
to come outside.

We sat in the ring of arborvitaes, alone and
smiling.

I took the ornamental ring from my pants
pocket and asked,

"Will you marry me?"

There was a short pause, I was glued to the
ground in quicksand-like gravity.
C smiled and said, "Yes!"

She looked jubilant and said she would keep the ring forever and never take it off.

We both looked at each other for awhile and then she said,

"I feel different."

I didn't admit it, but I felt the same. For some reason we were changed from the small experience. Things were getting serious now, and neither of us had the maturity to handle it.

The quicksand grip laid me down against the earth as I laid on the ground looking through the ring of trees at the stars above. I felt scared and overjoyed simultaneously.
We discussed the wedding quite a few times after that.
She would wear a tuxedo. Not being much for gender roles and loving to go against societal norms, it sounded perfect. My

parents weren't too sure about it, but she was a rebel in every way.

It was the happiest time of my life and I embraced it fully.
This was Heaven come to Earth and I could see a bright future ahead.

…Until the news came that would change my life and how I viewed the world forever…

Love Burns

"Honey, I love you."

"I love you too"

"Everything will work out"

The sobs echoed through the hallways of my psyche.

I heard her say, "I don't want to die."

It was mid January and the birds of the joyous summer had long ago flown South to seek refuge in the Sun's embrace.

At that moment, I could have used a little Sun, because the fire I so enjoyed sitting by was slowly burning to a semblance of embers.

The doctor said it was stage 4 Lymphoma. I had no idea what that was.

I asked the doctor, "Will she be okay?"

The doctor looked to his shoes and let out a
heavy sigh.

"We will do all we can."

I knew that my life would be forever altered
at that exact moment.
The waiting was the worst.
Waiting

Waiting

and Waiting

I stood hoping that blood test after blood test
that there would be some good news.

Charts at every turn

Aged people giving their final breaths

Death was a curtain I could no longer hide behind in this game of hide and seek we call life.

I held her hand during every hospital visit. The tears were never in short supply, and neither were the smiles. We were going to beat this as we'd beaten everything before.

Chemotherapy

....Beep....

....Beep....

....Beep....

The monotone noise of the heart monitor
was the only sound that night as I sat there
by her bedside. I hadn't really left her side
for but a few times to take care of my
affairs. Her hair was disheveled and she
smelled of masked sanitizer. I decided to get
up and kiss her forehead. At that moment,
she awoke and let loose one of her mind-
melting smiles.

I knew that everything would work out. I
didn't believe in a God, but I prayed
anyway.

I had faith in the fairness of the galaxy and
all who fell under its neon navigator.

2 months of keeping faith and constant reassurance to C that everything would be okay, left me sickened and tired. I hadn't eaten or slept well since the diagnosis.

The therapy eventually claimed her hair, but never her spirit.

She looked as luminescent as ever and the halo which seemed to surround her never faltered.
C had always believed in God. We often talked about what was out there, and what would happen after we died. I never believed in life after death, nor a God. She would point things out to me, simple things. She would say,

"See? How else could you explain that?"

"SEE?"

I would just mumble and shake my head.

I wanted more than ever this time for her to be right.

I had to be open to the possibility; that if anything happened to C, that I would be able to see her again.

The Bell in the Church of Christ

She died on a Saturday.

I still can't believe I'm saying the words.

Dead. Died. Gone. Poof!

Like some demented Hollywood Thriller,
my life was stalked and shattered.

And C….She was gone….

What had C done to deserve this fate?

What happened to this "Merciful God" that
she believed in?

I couldn't handle it….I had to get some
air….

I walked to C's church and told everyone the
news.

Devastation.

I retreated to the bell tower where I could
get a better sense of everything. I traversed
the stairs frantically, while wiping hot tears
from my eyes.

I got to the triangular room where the giant
bell was seated. I backed up against the wall
and collapsed my head into my knees. I
cried for what felt like hours.

The bell started ringing and I could see the
world below me through the open window.

For a split second, I felt like jumping from
the tower. But something inside my heart
grabbed me and pulled me to safety.

I was healthy and C wouldn't want me to
die. She would reassure me with kisses and
tell me that
everything will be okay; just as I had done
with her during her bout with Lymphoma.

I took a deep breath and walked back down the tower steps. I exited the church before anyone could see me and lit up a cigarette. For the next 8 days I stayed in my room and waited for the funeral.

Grave of One Thousand White Roses

The funeral was one of melancholy
celebration of the life once known as C.
The open casket revealed more than a
lifeless body; it revealed just how open
and vulnerable we all truly are. Behind our
egos, our bravado, our computerized
narcissism..we are all frail humans living on
borrowed time.

I walked up to C and looked upon her.

"I love you," I spoke softly.

For the first time since we met, there was no
reply.

I set one white rose on her suits lapel.

It was her wish to be buried in what would
have been her wedding attire.

If I had had one thousand White Roses, I
would have covered the graveyard in
response
to God for taking my favorite angel away at
such a young age.

Yes, I said it, God.

I guess she finally convinced me to believe
in a higher power, though now I looked
upon this power as an unjust beast who takes
what he wants and leaves the rest of us
behind.
I did have hope though. I had to believe that
I would see her again.

After the somber burial, I stayed when
everyone else had long gone.
I stood staring at C's grave. I knelt before
her tombstone and kissed it.

I ran my fingers along her name embedded
in stone and planted a kiss on the top
of her tombstone.

I knelt before the grave remembering the vows that I had written long before I ever proposed to her.

I said them aloud to the cold mound of dirt and stone.
"I promise to love you with every action and breath I take. I will hold you in my heart until Heaven and Hell break apart in the emptiness that becomes us. You were always the one, and no one could ever replace the fire in my heart you give me every time you smile…"

I stopped mid-sentence and began to silently cry.

I laid a poem I had scrawled before the funeral next to the flowers that her aunt had gotten her….

My Wish

I want to exorcise you
from the dirt
With my holy fingernails
tearing at your casket

I want to birth you back into
this world as if from a dynamite encrusted
womb attached inside my cherry-plumb
heart

I want to scream at you for
leaving me in this fallen Eden
filled with emotional, electronic malaise

I want to resuscitate the stars in your eyes
and wash away the formaldehyde handprints
that the coroner washed you with.

I want to close the gap between life and
death
and mostly…
I want to hear your voice again

"...I
want
to
hear
your
voice
again..."

www.ingramcontent.com/pod-product-compliance
Lightning Source LLC
Chambersburg PA
CBHW060539030426
42337CB00021B/4349